Immigrant

T0015106

STANLEY NELSON

IMMIGRANT

Book I

BIRCH BROOK PRESS

Other Books by Stanley Nelson
The Passion of Tammuz (Bellosguardo Press)
Idlewild (The Smith)
The Brooklyn Book of the Dead (The Smith)
Chirico Eyes (Midnight Sun)
The Travels of Ben Sira (The Smith)
The Unknowable Light of the Alien (The Smith)
101 Fragments of a Prayer (Midnight Sun)
Nightriffer (Birch Brook Press)
Driftin' on a Nightriff (Sub Rosa Press)

Designed & Printed at
Birch Brook Press
PO Box 293
Otisville, NY 10963

Monotype set & cast at
Out-of-Sorts Letter Foundry
Mamaroneck, NY

Sections of IMMIGRANT appeared
in PULPSMITH Magazine.

IMMIGRANT is typeset in 11 pt.
Kennerley and was printed with a
Miehle V-45 letterpress on 80-lb.
Mohawk Vellum.

*To my wife, Betty Jean—
who joined me on
The Immigrant Quest*

Reverie 1

believe

in the midst of urb   end
point of the dreamtime
                    im   pinging
               on my   dream
alarmtime brief
casetime animusly project
droptime

          on

               ah

outbreathe
on
          reverie   ah   reveries   reverie

          the entrance
walk of the apartment house
is composed of shalerock
of many hues: green, pink, salmon, blue:
but the idea is to
get from the entrance to the sidewalk
stepping *only* on the *black*
no easy task
since the black zigzags
around a flower garden set in the middle of the walk en
circled by a brick wall
                    how easily one can imagine

being lost in a castle
that it shall and may be lawful
for the freeholders and inhabitants

of the village residing near the ferry
within a line to begin   opposite to
and to be drawn up the road that leads from the still-house
including the same still-house
and the other buildings on the south side of the same road
to and across the road
leading to the ferry south of the house
and from thence north-easterly including all
the houses on the east side of the road just mentioned
to the place
of beginning would

                    you believe
in this   Veryurbanmidst
                    came a freight railroad
right down the center of Bedford Avenue
                              near Avenue J
where they started to build the tennis courts
see
      the claymixers rusting
                    in the sun
                              are they still
there
      if you played hooky
you could come here
you could sneak under the wire fence
and sit for hours
like a country rube
in the dry dust and tall weed and rock
of the railroad cut
counting the freightcars
bringing placenames of 'once rural America'
smell of distant modes
I can remember when they still had farms in this region

or was it someone older
who told me—my father? —there were farms
in this region
it must have been something I heard
in my childhood they turned off
the sprinklers in the park
did they ever turn them back

so imagine the anomaly of the freight railroad
where it is
imagine being lost in a castle
or a Coney Island funhouse
which is as scary as funny
                        and you can call this a place
abounding in otherness
                        let's call this a place
of otherness
                where aliens and immigrants and hooky players
                can come and be and make up their own mode of silence
                and everyplace outside this place
                whose boundaries we've just made up
                we'll call *alien*   but this is an over
                impingement of spirit   leaving too little substance
the world demands
                a *geography*
                        devolves in
                                specificity

And that is why I have located this *particular*
place
whose
geography is unknowable
                        but describable
                the rest will pretty much just happen hey

11

there's your bus I'll get on with you if you'll take it
to the end of the line too
late you're
gone somewhere
to go nother
time
these buses have funny numbers, ominous,
like numbering radioactive isotopes
AQ41   W63   AQ20   K117x
this one goes to
Gravesend Bay that's
the end of the line and we're not ready
for the end of the line
                        a place of endgraves a
                        mouth of waters
                    it's safer here mostimes
                it's hard to cut loose and just wander

in our shudderdreams

            we can invoke that terminus: here
        everythingends 'ass
                        hole of the Universe'
                                    reaching the boundary
of an aeon
            but we don't want to go there
            in our wakinguptime   so brief   so brief   much

safer here   gentleplace
                                    if you want it to be it
has an inland containment
                        there is so much to observe
                        without rushing, we're in no
                        rush

12

in this painting in the history book
a winter scene
how the villagers ingenuously
brueghel
building fires in the snow
in front of their woodframe houses
feeding the chickens and ducks
the painter, an Englishman on holiday, has caught
the comingling of chimney smoke and slattery sky
they called it a dirty place
even then
with cartways for streets
where the swine ran loose
'you will extricate yourself
'from the narrow, dirty, and disagreeable streets
'with all possible despatch
'and turning the first road leading up the hill,
'you will soon find yourself
'agreeably raised above the noise and dirt
'of this dull place, and moving along toward the breast of the hill
'you will have a noble and *near*
                                view of the city' (I am so happy

to be in this pleroma)
                           but see already
just by cutting loose
without thinking or caring
we've reached a new place, left behind
the place of history books and prerevolutionary fortifications
we reached this place before
on our rollerskates
maybe it was too far
maybe it was bikes
                          when did this

13

happen?

   when we turned the corner

        and there were

cobblestones?

     when we found the trolley tracks

where trolleys no longer run

       to nowhere? when we reached

the deadend

    in front of the boarded-up *cheder?**

    here

the streets are triangular

       pythagorean

           hermetically skeltering

in a zigzag of mishmash

      we could be afraid

we were told

    never to cross

    Foster Avenue

        we're across   our

rollerskates zipped us to the other side

sometimes the wheels get caught

in sewergrates

sometimes we have trouble stopping

the faces are different

the stores have different names

even the wind is different here

massive oaks in front of a tradeschool

this could be country

for someone who has never known real country

once this was

*Hebrew school

14

a furthestout place
retreat for preschool girls and nuns and mental patients
they had to extend the subway
reroute the buses
just before the war
the circus pitched its tents on these grounds
that wasn't too long ago
I heard it
from the men who told schoolyard epics
and played softball Saturday mornings

        Anne Greener
          you lived on this block
        little dutchgirl
          so blondpetite
          Anne Greener

        straight hair blonding
          your white assemblyblouse
        seventhgrade lips
          red as your assemblyscarf
          I saw you

        only on assemblyday
          prettiest girl in school
        pretty little dutchgirl
          you dazzled me
          every assembly

        day. Anne Greener
          you went to this church
        white clapboard
          with green shutters
          countrychurch

         like the railroad cut you
            don't expect to find
         you came to our school
         from so far
         away. I never

         (Anne Greener)   saw you

         after publicschool

KENILWORTH CHURCH
                    last of the lutherans
                              and presbyterians
the greeks moved in
finding the white sandstone houses
so much like ruins of Mykonos
Teddy Trias' father
had a display of grapefruit in the window of his restaurant
just grapefruit always
pyramids of grapefruit
on the lawn the bulletin board still says
services in latvian, german and swedish
neat tuliprows and hedges even
redmaple
so quiet here
only a wind carrying dust
from vacant lots
so faraway
from the tall buildings
always hurting our eyes
we never wanted to go, to leave
you could see the Empire State Building from our roof
only six stories high
they said we had to go

it was time
to cross the bridge and the river
the lady who lived near the ferry crossing was a Tory
informer
we might have lost except for the fog
the troops massed near the Plaza
where the baseball stadium

                    used to be I want
                    to go faster
                    we're going too fast when the whole idea
is to slow down
                    let's rest awhile in this courtyard
where the sun never trespasses except at angles
I do not want to speak of
                    courtyards, garter-
                thighed women on folding chairs

let's go to the schoolyard
we've brought along a softball   whole books could be written
about schoolyards,
                their love of children!   whole reveries

whole patersons

                    invoked!

it would take that genius
of the paterson mythmaker
and we have only meager tools
a Coney Island funhouse
a building with red turrets

                    like a castle

17

Reverie 2

And it
          did
                    and it did
                              have red turrets

this castle. This was before

we moved to the building
with an entrancewalk and flowergarden
encircled by a brick wall. If you take the BMT
across the Manhattan Bridge—you'll be
coming from there, I know—you can still see
that old castle, feel
its quakeandhover   old   castle
near the Kings Highway stop
hovering an outcropping
                              of yellowing rock (easy

to imagine its embrasures, machicolations) built
for bleakness except for the turrets
and the whole world beyond its counterscarp   no
conductor or overseer
will observe you
if you want to stand with your palms up
and watch the sunlight
filter through wooden beams
of an outdoor elevated platform. They, the overseers
or archons
          they   will think you just emerged
from one of the norman-arched panels against the subway wall
just tall enough
for medieval man

                    mother   my mother   come play

20

with me in the courtyard we know this courtyard
belongs only to children
my mother hands me a glass of milk
out of the first-floor window
she leans like a nude in an expressionist painting
but she is dressed in a shroud
We live their   (the souls)   death
and they live our death

                    I might have explored
its utherdragonheaded wallwalks and cellars and stairwells and passages
expecting to find a werewolfess in heat
clutching a mariafasa plant (which, as you know,
grows only by moonlight) there was always the smell
of steaming urine, someone
was always peeing in the radiator
for souls to become moist is delight or death
earthy
          earthy and moist
                    Castle by the Forest
                              Castle by the Sea
in the Coney Island funhouse
(we find our themes here and there)
you walk on squiggly stuff
it feels like the bones or tissues of ancient castlelords
doomed ordainers who die chained to a dungeonwall
crying out for Marion or Ygerne
but this is the New World
probably the tissues of postoffice clerks
the man who takes your ticket and stamps your wrist
is housecurlishly
churlish
blonde and roundskulled
with maroon headband

his soft strangely breasts bulge against a grape-colored teeshirt
the mechanical fatlady squeals and howls in her haha booth
but the tickettaker is morose
scratching on his biceps
the remnants of a badly removed tattoo
his buddy of the eternal toothpick
sprawls unshaven on a folding chair
guarding the entranceway
against the rush of stamp-wristed hordes
and the third overseer of the funhouse, a BMT conductor
before his leg was crushed between subway cars
stands on a platform in a baggy greensuit
barking through his cardboard megaphone
indecipherable instructions
these blunt squat giottoforms

must be the archons, the doorkeepers
they have the shape of creatures
who have bypassed millions of years of evolution
(like in H.G. Wells' Isle of Lost Souls)
toothpickman
motions to an empty cart
you sit next to a friend from publicschool
maybe Joe from Avenue H
you do not want to be near a stranger in a Coney Island funhouse

and you do not want to be pregnant or a cardiac risk   RIDE   RIDE
AT YOUR OWN RISK   *and ye*
who enter here   abandon   all hope   you

are entering the realm of Spark-a-rama
of
          Screechy Nell   Coffin Nanny
Jungle   Monster and his Human Mate   Jingle

Snake Dragon   **you**

are crossing the moat to Castle Frankenstein (o groovy groaning)
           and do villagers   still whisper
        in the heart of the forest their   regenerative shame?
                              the cart zaps

                    through rusty gates pitch
                    darkness and the cart   zapstirs
                    shakily

                    your face   pummeled
                    by sticky muckwick
                    what could it be probably

                    wetbread or bananas
                    just the same   stickypoopyuchearthymoisty
                    you see just the flashes

                    Gorilla's Hideaway and Hangman's
                    Delight   you see
                    not the monster but the monster's

                    reflection   you are witness
                    to something you could not have   neverever
                    witnessed   Beheading

                    of the Gaul and so you have
                    beenwitness
                    in a shudderdream   how

did we get here, leave
                the cart, enter
                              this dungeon of marauding mirrors?

23

like when we reached the deadend
found the deserted trolley tracks
                                                to nowhere
like when we couldn't control our rollerskates   *we were told*
never to cross Foster Avenue

now you are really on the squiggly stuff
hemmed in by strangers with blackened wrists
they do not want you to breathe
they are affronted by your breath and want to steal it
they want to contaminate your legs
with fear they want to violate

all over the place they
do not belong
at all

at all in your
pleroma so   escape   there has to be an escape route
every castlefunhouse has one
secret trapdoor or fake stonewall or
singlefile passageway secured by iron portcullis
that lifts if you can only find the winches
your passage to an open sea or sunlit valley
(this is all slapdashed from shudderdreams and B movies)

here you must depend on green footprints
dimly perceived between lightflashes
right out of a Teach Yourself to Dance mailorder manual
you trip over feet, your own and others, there seems to be
a turnstile in the distance
another tickettaker
but can you make it
you are suffocating in

24

swarmflesh
vertigo
     beckons

             you want your memories your
glass of milk   courtyard games   sewer stopped

        with popsickle sticks   I touched
     yoursleeve
           ring a lee vi o

emerge
     you have
     Emerged
       to new castlegrounds all luciform

and airy   ramparts
lightsoft   and their flags stir a
     welcoming breeze
           (someone took away the
           DEADEND sign)

       you have entered a new body
still your own
      is this radiance from without
     or a reflection of your own inner
      radiance   the radiance is
             You it comes from

    Otherness

        but is summoned
          from within *The physical*

being of man is but the outer impression of an invisible
subtle, more dynamic embodiment
of the soul   it has its seat in the innermost place
and enters the living creature   as it were   from a
                                                    Citadel

when you PUSH
the yellow button
of this stonefountain
you get an arc of water
that just reaches your mouth
you're big enough to drink by yourself
        it's easier if someone lifts you   but everyone's gone away

                        maybe they disappeared
                        when you folded your arms
                        against the schoolyard fence
                        and pressed your head
                        against your arms and shut
                        your eyes and counted to a
                        hundred
                                you're alone here this
                        placeof
                                eternalbeckonun
                        know
                                ablebut maybe just
                        maybe describable

alone and you don't mind   among these hedges like barbicans   those
                                                                people
    were a drag   you could look it up you could   dwell here

I am amazed at the light-wrapped
aura of this castle castles
are supposed to be

blackforesty
moory dour grey things
roundskulled villagers burn down every generation or so
the monster is totaled in the crumbling ruins
then discovered intact in a slab of ice by an uncle or stepbrother
lords and earls and uthers
drink methyglin round great wooden tables
roar and slam their flagons and demand their muttonchops plot
siege against every other castle
or plan the annual jousting tournament
gibbets hover, mangonels crepitate
dragons throw up serfs huddle
in cold wattle huts (what
is wattle?) deadacross the moor
snow and wind
split and blistered
rubble like stones in a vacant lot
                              they

              took away our vacant lot, the people
              who built the pink stucco house
              and blacktar driveway
              (we never saw them)
              where we built our forts
              and fed our cats
              and dug foxholes like the men

in the Big War
              but then

what do I know of castles   cobblestones
and synagogues maybe   a silo
but not castles my history
                              is discontiguous
              I am not familiar with

"one red rose is to be rendered"   I cannot distinguish
the Knights Templar from the Knights of St. John or
the Battle of Pinkie
from the Siege of Haddington   I have not memorized
the lyrics of imprisoned kings
for all I know
Freskin de Moravia was a juggler   I am disinterested in
the specific architecture of Welsh fortifications
though I love the word

                              ashlar

                                        I am from a people
                        dubbed discontiguous
                                        those castlegrounds
            I never entered except as magician or sorcerer or healer

and even this memory was lost
when we crossed the ocean
to a land without history

But look
while we've been talking and thinking of other things
we've come back to that old castle (see the red turrets?) near
                                        Kings Highway
we'll be safe

            here in this courtyard   where only children play
here we'll hunt the stag and hart
                feed cornflakes to the unicorn

                my mother is taking off her shroud
                and putting on on her housedress

she is so happy

                she is singing

28

Reverie 3

AQ41   BOX STREET WALL
        ABOUT AQ41
                            W63   AQ20   K117x
go buses go
crissycross

AQ41   BOX STREET WALL
        ABOUT
AQ41   BOX
                                        STREET   WALLABOUT
                    W63   AQ20   K117x

I made
    up   K117x

    there's really no bus like that
it's really a radioactive isotope
but there's really a B61 and B62
though I don't know the difference
they both run the same route

but one must have a different end of the
line
hey
go
with me to the end of the

it won't be the *end* of the line that asshole
of the universe
that place of endgraves
do you visit sometimes the graves
        of your parents?   I never do   I never have

        The stage left Gravesend in the morning

30

and did not return again until the night
The journey became, therefore, a matter of dread
rather than pleasure
for those COMPELLED
to take it: here

look at the map
see the red orange yellow navy blue cerulean
lines
each is a different route
separate unto itself

but there are maybe thousands of crossings
where you switch from one bus to another
without even trying
you could spend a lifetime
in this place we have called a place
Unknowable
that takes seven different colors
and a dozen different symbols

even to describe it
your final destination is posted at the front of the bus
If you go to the last stop
you can see the busdriver
alone in his passengerempty vehicle
rolling up one destination

31

and posting another

he might think it strange
that you are sitting in a parked bus
with no other passengers but you can think him strange
for posting and deposting destinations (as if

                          destinations can be scheduled)

you had no destination
on your bike or rollerskates
but this is different
they have told you this
the people who go in and out of the city
you see them with their maps spread
pinpointing exactly where they want to go
saying I'll leave at suchandsuch a time for suchandsuch a place
and get there exactly *on time*
on time

     what does this mean?
                  do we want to inspect the map?
        plot our course?
           Baedeker
               our route?

       more fun

       to just start out
       go to the end of the line
       or change buses

       and you don't have to pay
       another fare—

                    or get off
                    at any stop
                    and meander
                    without animus
                    this place
                    big enough

                                        to contain
                                        our meandering as it contains
                                                            itself
                                                    so scary

scary
so far from our schoolyard
so way past Foster
if you ride this bus
you see the busdriver only from back
his uniform his cap where it makes a redmark
at the back of his head his hand
on the big roundknobbed clutch who

are these people
                        waiting at the busstop?   fun
            house gang
                        followingstill with
                                        violative blackened wrists?
                the Coney Island Hellhole

looks like a funhouse ride
but a sign says: *this is not a ride*
you should go down to a hellhole
but you go up and up a wooden
curvingramp
you can't see what's ahead of you and the ramp is enclosed
by a steel frame so you can't see out ahead is
nothing

though you keep walking up and up and up
you are walking into the sky
not only the earth but the heavens above it
are in darkness
you are going up and up and up
then a teenager in a torn sweatshirt says:
'Don't you know about this ride?' *this is not a ride* 'You're pinned
against the wall so you can't move then they drop you
into total darkness'   the funhouse crowd marauds
downward on the ramp not one
has taken the ride that is not a ride
you want to keep going you want to go further you want to find out
but the crowd is against you
fearsomely
you are pushed ever downward
to exactly where you started
so this must be the unhell

hole nonride

today the villagers are
                              brueghelsome
                                        see them

down the block
                  from the busstop
                              bruegheling down to the docks

it's a block
            party or Antic or Frolic
                                        celebrating themselves

their block,
                  their neighborhood;

                                        they've strung banners

across the streets
                        treetop to treetop
                                        and set up

booths in the veryhover
                        of sodomgommorragod
                                        zilla   monster

                monstercity

of stony hardons and schmutzbelch
that other place that has no
otherness
lithuanian booth polish booth haitian booth gas company
booth CRIME
                PREVENTION IS YOU   Learn To Protect Yourself

At the Captive Nations Headquarters
they've built a stage right on the India Street docks
for a special performance of their own light opera company
the lead tenor runs the local bowling alley munch
italian sausage as you take in the aria
feel the evening baybreeze
children keep sliding on skateboards
rolling down sidewalks in cardboard boxes (the box

                        can be a bike
                        or car
                        or wagon for

                        one boy to pull another
                        it can be a house

                        35

or rocking toy

stood on its side
it can be a store
little girls use card

board boxes as dollbeds
or to stack up as a dollhouse
upsidedown they become tables
for makebelieve teasets

if you want a monstermask
you cut a hole in a cardboard box
when we went to the Farragut Woods
we used cardboard boxes
as sleds to go
downhill in the snow

the cardboard box can cover your head
when you have no cap or umbrella)
rev

olutionary times

the British held prisoners on a troopship anchored in the bay
commentators of the times
said it was worse than a hellhole
prisoners manacled and numbed and diseased
now the citizens

brueghel right down to the docks

faraway

how faraway this neighborhood seems
from the tennis courts and the freight railroad
Anne Greener's
KENILWORTH CHURCH
inland
containment, even the wind is different here
in the window of Teddy Trias' father's restaurant
pyramids of grapefruit just
grapefruit 'Two licensed hackmen

'with perhaps five or six extra carriages for weddings and funerals
'were able to furnish all necessary transportation
'to those citizens who were not provided with vehicles of their own
'or did not prefer to travel the roads leading to the remoter districts
'on their own stout limbs. A line of omnibuses, started around 1830
          or 1840,
'was so irregular in their timetables, and schedules so dated and
          unreliable,
'that they obtained little patronage: In the Eastern district,
'the first omnibuses were started by a Mr. Williams,
'a painter who lived on South Fifth Street, near Twelfth.
'Unlike the systematic management of the present line of stages
'the first omnibuses were drawn promiscuously through the different
          streets
'and straggling pedestrians picked up and conveyed
'to and from
          these districts'
               you know
                    you know

          your
               des
                    destination
                         destination

37

posted
        posted right there
            there at the top at
                the front
                    of your bus

            Again

                the day of the glowering sky

                in a region of city projects

this is the time to start on a bustrip in this
this Alien
            Alienplace
            on the day of the glowering
the
the slatter
            ly and smudgily   schmutzily*   pinkily

like the dirty punchball we hit with a broomstick
when our hands were too small for a softball

it's lonely starting out
all over again
but now the bus has pulled over
to the yellow line at the sidewalk
perfect ringalevio area
where cars are forbidden to park
the crowd is pushing and pushing
you on
they want *need* to go *exactly*

*dirtily

where the A61 blueroute bus promises to take them
you have no choice   busdoors baroque

ly unfolding
        to mount the two platform steps
        clutching EXACT   you must have it   EXACT

            CHANGE   and drop it
                                        in the coinbox

where it whirlpools down *kooshachung*
                                with all that other
exactly deposited
            change
            when the busdriver turns the handle
            the coinbox looks like a gumball
            machine

gas
        (the smells are unspeakable)
        acrid chemicals and moldy apricots
        and rubber raincoats all mixed up
        with the smell of unexposed film
        when you burn it to make a stinkbomb

hey how
did you sneak onto that seat
between the transitcop and the nurse's aide why
is everyone facing everyone else
is this a punishment
they're all going to an industrial park
whatever that is
no they're not getting off
it's the shopping center

so they're all going shopping
that's the purpose of a busstop, to go somewhere
in particular
but they've gone only a few stops
on the blueroute look at all those stops
still on the map
they're okay, these people,
are they okay

they might be okay
to be in our pleroma but see how their coatsleeves
cover their wrists?   they might
have blackened wrists eyes
without pupils   just whites
and the inner
eyelids turned so all the red shows
they might be ghouls, did you ever think of that
wandering graveyards because they can't find their parents' graves

you don't want to hear the conversation
of the transitcop and the nurse's aide
you want to be safe
in your veryown
                    pleroma
you don't want to be a ghoul
but you just like to huddle
within yourself
like huddling in a big safe mackinaw
you're no ghoul because you can see your reflection
in the buswindow
glimpses of a park,
                    a bay, an ocean
            flight of pigeons
                on a buswindow

40

like the flight of wild geese on a country evening
ragweed and goldenrod on a vacant
lot can be country for someone
who has never known real country

on that big vacant lot
near Kings Highway (it was
our castlegrounds) we roasted

small soft-skinned
potatoes on a cold winter
afternoon

and called them
"mickies." we built
our fires from ripped

old newspaper, box
crates, and other
lotjunk

the trick
was to throw in
the potatoes before you started the fire, then poke

them with a stick
while the fire died
down. the skin

came out all burnt
and black and charred—if you got some
in your mouth it tasted horrible.

but nothing was so sweetsoft

and warm on your tongue

as mickiemeat

it warmed you inside
and the fire warmed you outside
                              the bus was moving lightly, sunnily

quick stops and starts
but now it veers and swoops
with the long arc of a spaceship

we are going

veryfar
              verypast
              where we started
              each place   we have never been
              becomes
                        the furthestout place
we think this vacant lot, no, more than vacant
abandoned
lot
filled with
looseleaf books and ripped-up autoseats
must be veryfurthestout
                          for A61
                              but the bus
              heaves another darklongcoastering
                                        Swerve
                              so sharp to   Veer
                                        to   gulp
it's hard to see out the window
anymore where
              are we

42

```
                    want the bus to
stop                      stop
                      at nextvery yellow line
            we'll jump off fast the plat
                            form
            the bus goes vroomarounddowndound      a
                  and the bus goes and          round
                            we'll get off at the next
                      red
                            stoplight bus
                                  stop or no we'll
            crissycross another
                            bus or just plain
                                  walkaround
      miracle            miracul
                            ous          busdoors unfolding
            zip! we're off
                            like we zipped    cross Foster    Kent
Street
```

305 EVANS PA PER   PR D CTS   CORP. was this

```
            the address              I lived in
                            this walledabout neighborhood
                  after my mother died
                            this aunt on my mother's side
                  took me in
                  the entrance of the house was wroughtiron
it was a private house
                  we lived in the basement apartment
      this aunt had big breasts and always wore a black dress
            she had a little girl
                  and every night she put us in the tub together
            it was so warm and nice
```

43

I didn't stay there too long
                              the aunt was religious
                    she sent me to cheder I keep
              trying to remember those afternoons
                          of men in skullcaps, boys with payas
              Mr. Beer our Hebrew teacher
                                        was six foot six
                    to punish us
                              he picked us up
                              and banged our heads on the ceiling

C.L.I.C.K.
        INDUSTRIAL
                CENTER

But why
      am I alone
you shouldn't
                        be alone why
              is everything so still
                              in an industrial center
                    BEDT
            Eastern
                    District Terminal where
are the people   occupants
                              there must be
                    only these black dogs   who occupy
                              I used to see them
              hardy as the
                        weedsofthisplace

44

          some   the weeds
                                        grow likebecoming
                    trees
                         on vacant lots
            the street curves
                              and curves
                                        curvingbay
               on rotted docks piled
                              with dockwood
                  geometric
                  endpoint
                         sun
                         distancing
                                     an empty playground
                                     I am the only one
            on the big slide
            they make you hold on

                                     with both hands and bring
                                     both feet together on the rung

before they let you go on
to the rung above
it burns when your legs are bare
but it's fun to slide

                                        oddplace

            for a moviehouse

                              the ticket taker's
                              in her glass booth
                                        like the hahawoman
                                        at the funhouse
               but no one is going in
               and no one is coming out
                              freightcars

                         45

                                        are bedded down
                    in this field next to the sugar refining plant some

are turned on their sides, rusty and decayed
so this is where the sanitation trucks
go to sleep
and this is the terminal
where all the buses go to sleep
except
            I have been on the nightbus
                    the busdriver is
                            frozen
                                in darkness
                        you can't eversee
                            his face
            but he must see you in his big frontview mirror
                                            huddling

        in your seat it's
                        gotten so cold
            he must wonder are you really a bigperson
                    the windows are fogged
                        you cannot see out
                    only the motion of the nightbus

            vibes his hand on the bigclutch
        are you
                really the only one
                going to the end of the line of

    end

            graves
                    he'll take

                            46

```
                        you there
                        he's never
                        been there
                        himself
        at
              Alien
              Place                      not

        evernever

                        stops
```

I am waiting for the stagecoach in front of a nightwood. All around
something is howling, perhaps the wind. It is the
road to Castle Frankenstein. The villagers are excited again. They are
moving through the wood like aroused animals. They are holding clubs
and stakes and flaming faggots. They want to burn down
Castle Frankenstein, to kill the monster that eternally troubles
their children's dreams. Dimly in the distance
I hear the stagecoach, the coachman whipping his horses
to a frenzy. It almost goes by, then veers, stops. I tell the coachman:
'Take me to Castle Frankenstein.' Inside my sister is sobbing,
my brother is silent at the wheel of the car. We are going
to the nighthospital. Someone is dying. I know
because I am a bigperson. The villagers
have broken down the oaken doors. Castle Frankenstein
is in flames. Soon the monster
will hover on the rampart, plunge to his death, perhaps to be reborn
in future childreams.

Reverie 4

in
  be
    tween   ness
of   the   in
           be   tween

          time   tweeny

        twixt

     grades
        shifting
           aeons ad
    justing sefirot re-
             arranging
we can feel it in our limbs
and if we want it
hard enough
     we can each become
             Adam Kadman
    stretching out   (our limbs)   the morning
    Universe
yawning in the un
        cautionous kush
           making cosmos

        but you'd better
           watchout you
don't want to become a ghoul or
archon fixed
     forever never
        changing
it all depends on you
in the dreamtime you learned
your every gestureaction and maybe even

50

words
but that's inadequate, a defect
the bigpeople demand a specific geo
graphic
cal
Place
where
ever you are
they want you to map it all out
with names and numbers
there's a map in your briefcase
in a manila envelope stuffed in
with xeroxes of W2 forms you see
it's like
the buses W2   A62   K117x
so we've got to try it, you know
or they won't ever leave us alone
they'll always be beating on us
with their fists and knuckles and wrists
beating on the window
of Teddy Trias' father's restaurant
                           stas
                                    is   we're not
    gettingany   gettingany
                            place
  how
      some

  how have come
  to this park next to a hospital
                          barren
       outcroppings
            barest
grass of burnt yellowrust

like Georgia must have been after Sherman
except they say
this was a fort in revolutionary times
a wooded crest cleared of its timber
to make room for five small cannon
they say Washington stood here
and witnessed the rout and slaughter
of General Sullivan's forces by British and Hessian troops
along the Bedford Road
why didn't he intervene, send troops
because, strategist, that would have weakened
his main line of defense
they called it a fort (and they still
call it a fortpark) though it never really was
an Italian named Peter Caesar Albertini
was once the only Western settler
and there are still people
who remember farms in this region
but soon, so quickly
whole neighborhoods were overrun
by mobs of immigrants and aliens
with forged passports
many came to work in the nearby Navy Yard
that's when city planners got alarmed
they were searching for a phrase
like 'urban sprawl' they wanted to preserve
a hint of
        'once rural America'
        well what better
        way than to

plan a park
        the villagers were outraged who
needs it our

property values
but then they grew to like the park
and became accustomed to making great use of it

           'along these pretty paths
           'schoolchildren trundle their hoops
           'and dollcarriages,

           'or race and romp
           'while in the summer
           'evenings the benches

           'which stand at intervals
           'along the walks
           'are occupied by romantic couples

           'who whisper tender phrases
           'to the soft ripple of the leaves.
           'the two play

           'grounds
           'are favorite resorts
           'in the summer of croquet

'and tennis players . . .'

       dot   dot   de

                        dot but

then they reneged, the city planners
they were impressed by 'sudden influx
of lower socioeconomic sector'
which contributed to 'urban sprawl'
they chopped up the park
                     in whole lots

                    they needed to build projects, the hospital
              for new immigrants from Dixie and Latin America
        the villagers
                    were outraged our
                              property values mecca
           for real estate
                       operators
              and reallygrafty
                              speculators
              SELL/LEASE 'who needs
them they make good ballplayers but what

              else?' now the park is shrivelled up and ravaged
              people keep going in and out
              of the hospital
              but no one goes in and out of the park
              least not on weekdays
              and certainly not in the haze of morning
              when the fake gas lamps are still on

              the primal light, they say
              is simply too bright
              for finite eyes to behold

              except the groundskeeper
              spearsticking blown newspapers
              slamming them into his canvasbag   what

              they did   the planners
                    they built   a monument   at the veryvery
        crest where Washington stood   IN MEMORY OF THE
           11,500 PATRIOTIC AMERICAN SAILORS
           AND SOLDIERS WHO ENDURED CONTINUED
           SUFFERING AND DIED IN WALLABOUT

                              54

DURING THE REVOLUTIONARY WAR—1776–1782
THEIR REMAINS LIE BURIED IN THE
CRYPT AT THE BASE OF THIS
MONUMENT   O *how we cling*

    to atrocity

             and abomination

                    walledabout

       memories   who
ever visits the

         monument?   reads

                    the inscription?

we keep searching for the yellow button
PUSH of the stone fountain   but this park
has no stone fountain

         how can we deal
         with a fort that was not a fort
         and became a park that is not a park
         and overlooks
         a canal that was a creek
         (the map does us no good)
so it all must

      you guessed it
   be just like

       THIS IS NOT A RIDE   sit

sit on a bench on this breasty hillock

      Sonja   Lorraine ↗77
      -N-   76——
      Joe   "Pisces"

and see an outline of bridges and

             beyond   cubicular customs of World Trade, twin God
zilla footprints   crushing the earth, searing the sky   we will
          visit that place, someday   yes we will
off
                    in the immediate distance, at the park's
                    periphery
                    men in mackinaws and yellow hardhats
                    are standing next to an orange repair truck
                    what are they repairing there is nothing
                    here to
                    repair   if you had binoculars
                    you would see on the side of the truck
                    WELCO   *Don't Settle For Less*
                                        maybe they're just goofing off
                    (like us)   taking a coffeebreak or peebreak
                          or just listening to their

                    transistor
                              gazeglancing
                                        impassive
                    at a small figure on a long green bench at
                 the crest of what is left
                    of this fort
                                   park   today is in

                 betweeness

so we won't visit the canal
weeping in its muckbed like lascivious
Sophia

                 we can intuit
                              it all
          anyway

56

on Bond Street
the sun declines like spring
weeds and rusting autos
                 the black dogs   a thousand
      bodegas

O.Z. (handwritten illustration) *Gedney* — unit of General Signal (198)
O.Z.–195

        the shipping clerk leans against a fire hydrant
    as he rests
    we learn from a box on his handtruck that

O.Z. (handwritten illustration) *Gedney*

    is into

MALLEABLE IRON
ELECTRICAL FITTINGS
and that
        This

is a #1 Expansion Fitting

small

figure

    on a long green bench
   on the crest of what is left
    of this fort
        park
           merging decorationlike
  with the sparse appointments
            of this monument, tiny
    revolutionary cannon
         stone needle
and globe
    like the trylon and perisphere of the 1939 World's Fair I

never went
but I did get my picture
on the front page of the *Daily News*
flanked by my father and my cousin
Herbie
we were right up there in front
right by the barricade
of the Macy's Thanksgiving Day Parade
Herbie
   was a refugee
      refu

   gee Herbie and Jeanie

I forgot you came to live with us
after the holocaust
your strange orthodox ways, your father

Max, a poor schochet,* broke his cigarettes
in three pieces and kept them
in a little wooden box   Aunt Celia
liked to sing Yiddish songs and tap her foot

blond-haired and blue-eyed as any Aryan
Herbie I wrestled you all afternoon
and dueled you with ashcans and woodbroom swords
but O Jeanie I loved your pale

refugeeness, I tried to learn the Hebrew prayers
for your sake (candles, white
tablecloths) and even a bit of German
but I could never be your mensch and besides

we were first cousins
I keep mixing up Aunt Celia the refugee
with Aunt Celia of the black dress
with my mother who was also named

Celia

* ritual slaughterer

59

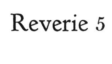

Reverie 5

I.

A

Shape   a Body   emerges
    villages/neighborhoods   home
for immigrants and aliens   medievalists, kabbalists, gnostics
might well remark
how the neighborhoods take shape
and verge one on another   forming tissues, veins, organs
yet each isolate and self-functioning
within the schema   *blood is the vehicle of the spirit*

it's hard to tell
where one neighborhood begins and another ends
maybe when we crossed Foster we got lost
forever
our rollerskates wouldn't stop we got lost
forever
our rollerskates wouldn't stop our bikebrakes
stopped functioning   it used to be
in the dreamtime

when we rode our bikes
we asked the kids playing in the streets what
public school do you go to
and that's how we judged how far we were from home
by the number of public schools
we passed P.S. 152 P.S. 130 P.S. 62 when you
passed three or four
that was a long trip and you had to rush home

for your supper
then it was also fun to ride
the bikepaths
on the parkway   in the Farragut Woods   in the park
the parkway was once called the Boulevard it was lined
with stables and large grounds trotting
races were held here every Sunday afternoon

    you see once we crossed
    how hard it is to stop   look here
        with me I won't   hurt you   promise   see
    on this jigsaw puzzle they've made into the shape
    of our Place
    how you could change and rearrange whole neighborhoods
    even individual blocks
    and it would still come out the same how
    you always begin and end at the verysame
    Place
    you have to be responsible in the dreamtime
    remember that it's almost godlike

to rearrange geography
see how the artist has dressed up his creation,
the jigsaw puzzle, given each neighborhood
its appropriate visual symbol
a BMT station   an owl's head   a cemetery   a pylon
    an aquarium   a huge hotdog
and he's (the artist, George Gorycki) even written
down some of the original Dutch and Walloon
placenames (Waal-boyt from the Walloon)   look

on the jigsaw puzzle   how much easier
to see the sprawl of everything
than on those paper maps you fold up like booklets

bursting with berserks of indices, appendices
all gargoyled with grids and numbers
and they make such a wad when you stick them in your backpocket
but the puzzle, once assembled
shows us each neighborhood as in a radiant light

open, white, smooth, untroubled
as it must have been as it must be
in the dreamtime   we've tried, man, how
we've tried to stay here right
here in the dreamtime
which is the time
of noncondition which
is
the time of nonform   and nonproject   and nondetail   and
        nonproportion and

nonprojection and nothing whatsoever
in your briefcase
but also the time of greatest responsibility
when your every gesturemovement
commands a Universe
how you stand up, how you lie down, how you sleep and wake
        what's
going on
on on   in
side you, my man, it's an inner-determined ritual
imposed from within
you don't have to show it off to other people if you don't want to
you can show whatever you want
and keep the rest for yourself
let them be the showoffs
we'll stay safe and cozy

here in the dreamtime   each of us
supports a Universe   imagine (like
the freight railroad) a Universe   depending
    depends on each single one of us
they don't understand
            they've got the schedules stuck in front of their noses
        they want to take command
                            the big people
    so let them have that outer hunk so who cares they

won't let you live or be
without animus
they want their forms and norms a re
capitulation   an objectification   a resume
neatly typed and double spaced how did you
(of all people) come to write this? did you get the idea
from a book? why do you want to do this
anyway? why can't you be happy like we are happy
making charts and grids and graphs and schedules? There

is a man who will sell you real estate. Good property can be sold.
        But to
sell it quickly somebody must do some hustling.
    Most owners cannot do this for themselves.
    Most of them don't know of anybody they can get to do it for
        them.
    Of course they have plenty of real estate men.
    Their name is legion.
    But "listing" property with a real estate man is one thing.
    Getting a broker who will sell it is another thing.
    Many owners think that is just the kind of service a real estate man
ought to give them.
    But it is not the kind they get.
    And they have no right to expect it.

65

This may be a new idea but it is a fact. Now you see

this is a clear, direct, purposeful statement. It makes its point, while
                                        your grammar
is inadequate; you keep mixing up
tenses and attribution and why can't you sum it all up
in one or two aptly chosen images? we can't

explain, they won't listen
how edges wound us, splinters
pierce our soul   how we can't contain
our grammar and tenses not knowing
even if what we selected from wads of scribbled pages
is apt or right or revealing or instructive here
look   in my notebook I'll   let you   it won't
    hurt   which is the same as looking in my soul
here look where I've written "This is all a mishmash
of luncheonettes and lost notebooks"   luncheonettes, yes,
and lost notebooks but also queasy
bowels   I was sitting at the very time
in a luncheonette drinking hot coffee and looking out
at the backstreets behind the hospital
near the park
which is not a park

the windows are fogged
the people look out
at a vendor
peddling grapes from a white wicker cart, the other vendor
peddles sweatshirts
and wraps his scarf around his head
in between the grapes and the sweatshirts
appear the backstreets of the hospital
like incisions on the brow of Frankenstein's monster

made by the stepnephew who has priesed him out of the iceblock
and set him on the white operating sheets
and turned up the electromagnetic circuitry to its full strength
so the gadgety wires and doodaddy sockets and fluorovescent panels
screech and sparkle and magicalize
the stepnephew wants to see what makes the monster tick,
to bring him back to life, but in that radiant preorgasmical
moment when he raises the scalpel
his hand becomes unsteady, his courage unsure
spirit is precisely the borderline
between reason and unreason, between body
and bodiless

also the streets resemble
the cobblestone alleys behind the gothic castle
where Dr. Jekyll hung his shingle and drank ale
with Toddy McFarlen and the gravediggers
(this is all from B movies)
they are more like the streets of the transit map
than the streets of the jigsaw puzzle

no patient has ever been on these streets
here they say the night orderlies
distribute the remains of monster fetuses
but that's only a rumor
told by oldtimers at the public market,
truck dispatchers and platform loaders
who work the nightsprawl and know about shudderdreams
it will always be a wonder
how the park found its way into our reveries,
the creek and the canal, we don't

ever want to force it
we want it to come straight out of our wrists

like blood
to shine from our eyes the lids
even, a
lightfix, so much to be in our breath
we want to tell confessionally
all there is to tell
and not go too slow or too fast
and not leave anything out, you see,
that's more important
even than the breathing or the poetry   you've been there

                you know it's the truth
about the Coney Island funhouse
and the ferris wheel that goes woosh above the beach
                you have your choice
of the red ferris wheel that doesn't swing
or the white ferris wheel that swings
                which you choose
because of that one great swoop
where you feel you've been launched and accepted into the sky
                that's a ride, man, a *ride*   trolleys

        deadends   we put pennies
on the tracks and rode the backs of trolleycars
and of the nightbus of the nightbus
oh how much to tell
the busdriver's pal
sprawled on the frontseat
wearing only a windbreaker
chewing on a toothpick
he always got off in front of the brewery
and dropped a manila envelope through the mailslot

In the summer people sat on Autenreith's open porch

ordered pitchers of beer and listened to the music
each cabaret had its own band or at least a piano player
the whole area was filled with music
especially in the summer

the music could be heard blocks away

II

Today

is snowy
        we will go to the sea, to what we know
        as the sea, ocean

    they sail on the moist, the dead souls

of perpetual flux   ever-becoming
for now we have grown tired

of inland containment, dust
of vacant lots, tuliprows
and redmaple
and the restaurant window piled with grapefruit
no fear anymore why
                should we be afraid
                of our origins
                to search to explore/explorers

make notable contributions, we learned that from our history books
Fifty Famous People
sitting in the backseat of the class at P.S. 152
and dreaming of Anne Greener

white shirts, white blouses, red
assembly scarfs it should be

very simple, to go to the sea, to find
natural water, we are surrounded
by water, ocean, rivers, creeks, canals, bays, channels
handball courts
are often built on playgrounds near the shore
we want to leave our bodies
what has become/will become
of our bodies   leave
The Phrygians call Him also Dead—when bound in the body
as in a tomb or sepulchre   our bodies
filled with attribution, inland dust   to invade

a new pleroma, the sea
will bring us there the great

                    Windsaltslanting

          this should be very simple, to get to the sea
          we've spied docks and piers right down the block
          and the shimmering waters from the buswindow

this is a land after all
storied by the sea, whales and sea captains
                              adventurer/explorers
(Mrs. Haas assigned us Moby Dick
and it was even better in the classic comic) land

of immigrants, we had the sea in our bodies
not like sailors or sea captains
but huddling within ourselves, hearing the oceanlap
in the vinegar-odored steerage

those who came before us
were more familiar with the land and its waters
they told of a great Father of Waters
pushing across the heart of a continent
made mythologic
by 'red savages' and white settlers
epics and talltales
of brawlers and rivermen
(remember Mike Fink
from the history books?) rafts,
steamboats, the life
of a great river and the great forests
surrounding it, wild, racoonish woodsmen
and later the homesteaders
setting down roots
in the heartland soil   this

was 'once rural America', if you belonged
you were trueblue American more
American even than the original Americans
but so remote
from those 'give me your tired, your poor, your huddled masses' folk
huddling in steerage, menagerie
of swarthy tongues, so
what if they were bilged and conscripted and indentured
and bought the Brooklyn Bridge
they dreamed America America
                    in the dreamtime
                 vast as it could be ocean only
                                  intimate
                          as in a reverie
          let's
              go find it, me
              and you and anyone

else who cares to come along
         sea of access, sea of arrival, sea of exodus, an
nunciationous young
                 strong sea as in
those ghettodreams, it must have been
burned for those immigrants and aliens
                           who never laid real eyes on it
                           squiggling between idle snowplows
              we can turn down Sackett Street
              a Filipino neighborhood Filipinos
              must have come from across the sea 'the original

'deed is held by a descendant of the Denyse family, now living
'on Eighteenth Avenue. It presented Denyse deed property
'May 13, 1807   April 28, 1785, Messrs. Simon, Jacques and Isaac
'Cortelyou sent 600 prime shad as a donation to the New York
'Almshouse. Their united business was the fisheries
'by the Narrows   April 16, 1791, a draft of shad taken from
'the Narrows waters were 14,000 fish
'and were valued at upward of £200   April 13, 1793,
'Isaac Cortelyou had a house of four rooms to let
'near bathing and fronting the Bay below Denyse's   May 2,
'1799, Transaction of land matters, between James Boyce, his wife,
'Sally, of Gravesend, and Denyse Denyse of New Utrecht.'
                  Document signed JAMES BOYCE (his X)
                               SALLY BOYCE (X)

'. . . not a dock large enough to receive the Olympia which came in
today—they mean there is no dock over in Manhattan large enough
to receive it. And there appeared that little mermaid or queen of
Gowanus and presented me with a bouquet of lilies as if to indicate
that the waters of the Gowanus, so bad-smelling and corrupt
heretofore, are to become pure as the white lilies presented me.
Even with the bad smells, it's not such an unhealthy place to live

after all. I don't know what Dock Commissioner Tapleau would do
if there were no Gowanus Creek. He would not know where to put
the coal and the sand and the building material and the oil

'and the things we have going up the river today' our own
world of water, aside from geography books
has been more like the creek of Dock Commissioner Tapleau
than the Narrows of the Cortelyous
how did we find our way
into this zig   mash   zag
we were heading down Sackett Street, sidestepping
snowplows
and Filipinos heading for the Corregidor Bar
it should be right ahead, right down the block
a short walk, simple
right past the renovated cheder
strange the sea approaching
but no seasmells
(oh a gull Vs over a water tower)
only a smell of synagogue benches
and diagnostic equipment
BENOV YAKOV SCHOOL
CENTER FOR DEVELOPMENTAL DISABILITIES
how did we start for the sea
and get to a yeshiva and a medical center? This
always happens, this seamirage
they're always putting in more landfill
extending us further from the sea
them   the same ones who sell real estate
and parcel up parks
and run the Coney Island funhouse
and slip manila envelopes into mailslots in the middle of the night

we can see the white masts and funnels

just past brown earth embankments
and snowy playgrounds
(they've fixed it so even snow
doesn't bring a season)

maybe if we turn down Van Brunt Street   Van Brunt
a name storied in American history?   maybe not but
in our pleroma
it's important   we're responsible
for Van Brunts and Van Brunt Street 'the Van Brunt family
'has been a scattered family of old homesteads. Each branch
'has been puzzled to know about the other branches,
'while the historic homesteads known to be Van Brunt homesteads
'have been just as mixed up as the genealogies. But certain it is,
'whatever the genealogies, there were three
'Van Brunt homesteads in the village during the 1775 war
'and along the Shore Road, between the Narrows and Yellow Hook.
'This homestead later became the property of the Crescent Athletic
        Club.'

this is a neighborhood where two rivers meet
becoming bay and channel and basin and ocean
you can see an outline of islands,
big white ships almost nonmoving like ghosts, almost
hear the prows
scraping in their docks but
how to get there   walk, rollerskate, bike?
maybe if we inquired at the
        OFFI E   someone could direct us
give us exit from this place of eternally empty warehouses
        GODZILLAVILLE
                        abounds
        boxcars piling up   impassive   cars stalled on icy sidewalks
fume   exhaustchemvalve   garbage   *garbage*

74

is sanitation
                    here the groundskeeper
has a wheelbarrow, he is wheeling oily rags
his companion, a young black, carries oily rags in a paintcan
and screams to his attackdog: C'MERE SLICK!
I GONNA KICK YOUR ASS!
we have come to the veryend
of Van Brunt Street
                    without access to the sea
          why is the sea cut off
                              by rusting autos
                    attackdogs
          and the wire fence of BENTON FIBRE DRUM CO?
     the villagers don't seem to care
they brueghel in the snow in mackinaws and boots
and caps with blue, pink, white, green pompoms
shaking their pompoms in the middle of Van Brunt Street,
throwing snowballs at the windows of novelty shops and finance
          companies
once we came here by mistake
(we meant to bike to the Farragut Woods)
and saw a woman in a torn dress
picnicking with two small children
on a vacant lot between the warehouse and the pier
they were sitting on fruitcrates
enjoying their milk and girl scout cookies

we have no choice but to turn back
toward the region of city projects
hey wait we'll
give it one more chance under
pass
ominousan
imus

75

on these little streets under the highway
lives breathes a great ship terminal
                    BEWARE
    THIS FACILITY   CIUDADO ZONA
    PATROLLED BY   VIGILANDA
    ATTACK DOGS   POR PERRUS
                                POLICALUS
      PARK AT YOUR OWN RISK

   OTHERS
      WILL BE TOWED AWAY   also
      we are blocked off by green wooden shanties

         extending out onto the pier and landfill
         the terminal is like a complex of municipal buildings
         you can't find your way in
         and you may never find your way out
             we don't want to be alarmed
             by attackdogs or towed away
         this must be allmirage
         the sea and the ships

unloading in their docks   terminalmen
do their work in secret, under the row of green shanties
materials are funnelled
from the first shanty built out on the landfill
to the last shanty attached directly to the terminal
outsiders are discouraged
only one, the luncheonetteman, is welcomed
because he is bringing pizza and coffee
you imagine them in plastic yellowsuits,
orange vests, maybe headlighted
hardhats, unloading and moving materials
with thongs and ropes, spokes, cargohooks, mechanical platforms

JUGO

LINIJA   JUGOLINIJA
  jab
    berwockyjug   gernaut
I cannot name or ken un
    holy tentragrammaton
sometime in the dim mist of past aeons a mutant of the great ship
terminal split

  off and dup
    licated and jugolinijad
  into this monsanto montage
      like a colony of rollercoasters self-
  replicating
  schmutzbelch and chemical fumes
  twin monster*things*
    we nightmared with our erector sets
  but could never build
    in these monsterlaps
      the white boxcars, huge in themselves,
    pile up like tiny toy trucks
  learn to drive a tractortrailer   I

cannot will not describe this this
        is a lost notebook write
a composition
or make a list
of the things you did today:

     1. we went to the sea

     2. we came to a terminal

Reverie 6

You deserve

now, my friend, a sunnier
mode. return
to inland containment. seasons, time of day, light and air
like my Uncle Strool/Aunt Rose's sixth floor
apartment overlooking the college campus. six floors,
the highest you could build on that swampy soil
twice as high as our own place on East 26th Street,
it was so high! you could just make out
the Empire State Building without going up on the roof.
when you opened the window, how the white curtains

blossomed in the air, columned in the light! I loved to sleep over
at Uncle Strool/Aunt Rose's. vegetarian Cousin Jack
did a great koussatsky after schnapps and spongecake. it's up to you,
returning. I want to. I want to go back,
never escape the freight railroad on Bedford and J,
the unfinished tennis courts (they'll never finish)
the schoolyard, courtyard of garter-thighed women
even the castlehover near Kings Highway. you stayed with me
through the shudderdream and nightsprawl,
the A61 bustrip and inbetweeness and hellhole ride. so

you deserve to cut loose and just wander a
gentleplace
if you want it to be. we can control feelings of
sentiment, of nostalgia, but cannot refuse
to mark them down. we can define, be definitive,
tuning out metaphysic. we can do this, make up our own rules,
our own mode of silence; everyone outside these boundaries we've
        made up
we'll call *alien*. much here is as it was. the candystoreman
is still there in his flannelshirt and white apron,
though he won't recognize you in your pinstripe suit,

carrying your briefcase and your raincoat neatly folded on your arm.
the cleaningstore man had a common-law-wife. are they still there?
the cleaner's is. kids still ride their trikes and bikes where they're
        not supposed to,
hang out on the high school steps, steal baseballs from the college field.
if you don't make it over the low wire fence, the groundskeeper
gets you with the knobbed end of his pick, sometimes
slapping your knuckles white just as you make your drop. during
        football season
they set up makeshift stands
on the roofs of six-story buildings across from the field. the
        movie theater
where we watched Boston Blackie serials

and old vaudeville Saturday afternoons
is now a banquet hall, but they've kept the marquee and appointments.
they've ripped out the many-colored shalerock from the entrance
of our old apartment house, poured in solid white concrete, but kept
the flower-garden encircled by a brick wall. how can we play our game
of stepping only on the black? this was the second place we lived—
after fire gutted the first floor apartment
on Kings Highway where each nice evening
my mother handed me a glass of milk; all the brown
European photographs were destroyed. even in our youth,

even before we were children, they changed
Glenwood Road School to P.S. 152. I wanted to sit
behind Anne Greener but they put me behind Maureen McCurdy.
Mr. Beishem our principal had a clubfoot. Mrs. Bois the music teacher
kept a mirror on her piano to see if the class was singing.
you couldn't raise your hand in Mrs. Connelly's class: if you had to
        leave the room
you put a note in her 'little gold box.' Mr. Gladding the shop teacher
spoke with a Scottish burr ("drrrillbit"), ate oranges whole and spit

81

the core and pits onto the floor
with the wood shavings. and what, my friend,

of the freight railroad? they've put in a new wire fence,
higher and sturdier, and walled up the space between the viaduct
        and embankment
but you can still sneak under. ask the high school kids
from the neighborhood and they'll tell you the trains still run:
        testament
to this strange mode of reportage: you can still play hooky
and count boxcars. we sense a resistance here
of places that are contiguous but not "a part of." the town resisted
the borough and the borough resisted the city. but they wanted
interlockedness, "arteries of commerce," the bigmacher
bigpeople real estate juguggly jugolinijars,

so it happened. but the resistance is still there,
the quaintness. maybe the massive oaks
in front of the trade school, or the wind
bringing the smell of distant modes, seed of lilac
and redmaple, hint of birdsong and seawatery places.
the quaintness has long been remarked on. the speech, the trolleys,
the baseball team that left town. some never went much
to the stadium (it's a housing project now)
it was too far away, way
past Foster. you can find it too in the history-books. 'They not
        only frowned

'on public improvements but even in their own homes lived but
        little different
'from methods followed by their ancestors.' 'Taking our leave,
'we rode on to 't Vlacke Bos, a village
'situated about an hour and a half 's distance from there, upon the
        same plain,

82

'which is very large. The village seems to have better farms than
      the bay
'and yields fully as much revenue. Riding through it, we came to the
      hills,
'which are very stony and uncomfortable to ride on.' The English
came later, in groups or colonies from Connecticut or Massachusetts
      Bay,
but the original Dutch wandered in as individual settlers,
many from the Old Country. Docile and tranquil,

they made their peace with the Indians
and had no massacres. when the Sachem of Rockaway—
one Eskimoppas—claimed a large tract of land, they arranged a
      barter: the land
for ten fathoms of black wampum, four coats, five blankets,
      two guns, two pistols,
five double handfuls of powder, five bars of lead,
ten knives, two aprons, one-half barrel of strong beer,
three cans of brandy and six shirts. farms
were laid out into 48 lots or tracts of land, extending
      600 Dutch rods
east and west on the Indian path,

each being an average width of 27 rods. justice was discharged
by a shout (public accuser) and two or three scheppen (jurors):
October 5, 1669. Shout complained against the defendant
for carting in buckwheat on a Sunday with his wagon. condemned to
      pay costs.
during the Revolution, the villagers 'expressed their intention of
      remaining neutral.' it's said
they never sent a delegate to the Constitutional Convention no patriot
or statesman emerged here. after the '76 War
the village 'once again relapsed into its slumbrous existence.'
      on the surface

this place has no attraction other than its quaintness. only oddballs
      like us
wander the dreamtime. and when that mood is on us,

tuning out chitchat and data,
we feel we might penetrate to the core of every pebble.
      sophomoric, yes,
worthy only of a Meyerink or Plato or Blake
or even Whitman. much depends on our approach. if we take the bus,
we get off at East 26th Street, walk down Glenwood Road
(see how we are definite and keep within strictures)
walking past the cleaner's and candystore, Uncle Strool/Aunt Rose's
apartment house, the white clapboard church. this time
we'll take the subway route, getting off at Nostrand and Flatbush,
kicking cinders along Campus Road

until we get to the college fence. we won't climb over,
just walk through the entrance. we have to take a detour
to sit on this bench. lilacs
just flowering in neat arranged stands
semicircled in wooden planks and based in brick. elm, maple,
      the ever-present
ailanthus. no matter that our little oasis
faces the student cafeteria where waitresses bustle
in black and yellow uniforms. apropos
of this place where a quiche emporium is across from
THE HOME OF EX-LAX. let's reverie. let's pause. let's

relapse awhile.